Shanmuganathan Vasanthapriyan
M.I. Isham Mohamed

Personalized Outdoor Audio Tour Guide with Augmented Reality

AF153240

Shanmuganathan Vasanthapriyan
M.I. Isham Mohamed

Personalized Outdoor Audio Tour Guide with Augmented Reality

A research on why and how to digitalize the Sri Lankan tourism industry to comply with latest technical trends

LAP LAMBERT Academic Publishing

Impressum / Imprint

Bibliografische Information der Deutschen Nationalbibliothek: Die Deutsche Nationalbibliothek verzeichnet diese Publikation in der Deutschen Nationalbibliografie; detaillierte bibliografische Daten sind im Internet über http://dnb.d-nb.de abrufbar.
Alle in diesem Buch genannten Marken und Produktnamen unterliegen warenzeichen-, marken- oder patentrechtlichem Schutz bzw. sind Warenzeichen oder eingetragene Warenzeichen der jeweiligen Inhaber. Die Wiedergabe von Marken, Produktnamen, Gebrauchsnamen, Handelsnamen, Warenbezeichnungen u.s.w. in diesem Werk berechtigt auch ohne besondere Kennzeichnung nicht zu der Annahme, dass solche Namen im Sinne der Warenzeichen- und Markenschutzgesetzgebung als frei zu betrachten wären und daher von jedermann benutzt werden dürften.

Bibliographic information published by the Deutsche Nationalbibliothek: The Deutsche Nationalbibliothek lists this publication in the Deutsche Nationalbibliografie; detailed bibliographic data are available in the Internet at http://dnb.d-nb.de.
Any brand names and product names mentioned in this book are subject to trademark, brand or patent protection and are trademarks or registered trademarks of their respective holders. The use of brand names, product names, common names, trade names, product descriptions etc. even without a particular marking in this works is in no way to be construed to mean that such names may be regarded as unrestricted in respect of trademark and brand protection legislation and could thus be used by anyone.

Coverbild / Cover image: www.ingimage.com

Verlag / Publisher:
LAP LAMBERT Academic Publishing
ist ein Imprint der / is a trademark of
OmniScriptum GmbH & Co. KG
Heinrich-Böcking-Str. 6-8, 66121 Saarbrücken, Deutschland / Germany
Email: info@lap-publishing.com

Herstellung: siehe letzte Seite /
Printed at: see last page
ISBN: 978-3-659-59029-0

Personalized Outdoor Audio Tour Guide with Augmented Reality- Sri Lankan Context

Authors:
S. Vasanthapriyan & M.I.Isham Mohamed
Department of Computing & Information Systems
Sabaragamuwa University of Sri Lanka
PO Box 02, Belihuloya
Sri Lanka

Abstract

In recent years, research on location based services has attracted huge attention and a wide interest due to the wide applications. Increased used of smart phones and GPS are the most important factor for this attraction. Meanwhile Point of Interest (POI) are more interesting research area with the location based services enabled world. Generally "Point of Interest" is a specific point location that someone may find useful or interesting. Furthermore, personalization is a very key concept in modern smart phone applications, which involves using technology to accommodate the differences between individuals. This research proposed a future concept called "Personal POI Recommender System with Social Data" that is a location based system, takes a user's personal points of interests from social data, notify and recommend him about those places for time to time.

This system analyzes social factors like Facebook likes, Facebook check-ins, Foursquare check-ins, Location data of user's tweets and his public, private status updates social network [1] sites such as Facebook, Twitter, Google+, Instagram and etc. This system store all the collected and analyzed data from Social networks sites in local storage of the device as an XML format. Then, this get users location and time and weather of that particular location and push notifications about nearby interesting places according to users like. A user can store his preferred places in this system as well. That is also stored in the XML file as a whole, we propose a better platform for Personalized Point of Interest services based on Social networks and user preference.

Personalized access to cultural heritage information attracts the attention of many researchers and practitioners. A variety of applications can be found for cultural places, such as museums, cities. The focus of this paper is more specially, on World Heritage city guides to be used by locals and tourists to make them understand what makes the WH property outstanding. Some very interesting though non-adaptive mobile guides have been developed over the past years e.g. mTrip, Pocket Guide.

However with the emerging usability of Augmented reality, people can easily find the places where they need to reach. But the current problem is there are still many researches carried out to find the best possible way to give a solution for personalized outdoor tour guides. This project provide such solution for the problem.

---

[1] a dedicated website or other application which enables users to communicate with each other by posting information, comments, messages, images, etc.

i

Contents

1 Introduction   **1**
   1.1   Over view of organization 1
   1.2   Business Process 1
   1.3   Definition of the problem 1
   1.4   Need Analysis 2
   1.5   Aims and objectives 3
   1.6   Scope of the system 3

2 System Analysis   **4**
   2.1   High level diagrams for existing system 4
   2.2   Methodologies used for the system 8
   2.3   GUI Design 10
   2.4   Program Design 17

3 System Development   **19**
   3.1   Brief description about the Developing environment tools & programming language . . 19
   3.2   Security Infrastructure 21
   3.3   Data Structures & Algorithms used in the system 21
   3.4   Implementation of Algorithm 21
   3.5   Augmented Reality Algorithm 23
   3.6   Saving User Preferences 33

4 System Testing   **35**
   4.1   Testing methodology used 35
   4.2   Test cases and Test results 37

5 System Implementation   **39**
   5.1   Implementation Requirements 39
   5.2   Installation guide 39
   5.3   User manual 39
   5.4   User Training 44

6 Discussion & Conclusion **45**
   6.1 The degree of objectives met 45
   6.2 Usability, Accessibility, Reliability and User friendliness of the system 45
   6.3 Limitations and Drawbacks 46
   6.4 Further Modification and Enhancement 46
   6.5 Conclusion 46

List of Figures

2.1 Abstract of scenario in users perspective   4
2.2 Abstract of scenario in systems perspective   5
2.3 Use case diagram for the system   6
2.4 How Augmented reality works   7
2.5 Agile Methodology to develop the system   8
2.6 Home page   10
2.7 System's main map   11
2.8 System's main map, showing recommended places, nearby   12
2.9 Augmented Reality, this uses camera's view port to show the places   13
2.10 The app showing a far places which is included in the users preferences   14

3.1 Visual Studio 2013   20
3.2 Sample XAML code, coded in Visual Studio 2013   21

4.1 V model testing   35

5.1 Main screen of the app on launched.   40
5.2 Showing the palces which are listed in user preferences   41
5.3 Showing a place   42
5.4 Showing the list again   43
5.5 Showing another place   44

List of Tables

4.1 Test case on saving and manipulating user preferences 37

4.2 Testing Augmented Reality 38

1

Introduction

1.1 Over view of organization

The huge availability of mobile and handheld devices such as tablets at present makes adaptive mobile guide apps in various domains including tourism. There are several GPS enabled "tour guide" and "story teller" apps available in all major smart phone and tablet platforms. Recently, Story teller apps have gained more focus from a huge users base. Instead of just guiding users from an app, we can recommend them to take pictures about beautiful views in those places. Combining Navigation apps and Story teller apps are a great idea yet to be implemented.

Personalized access to cultural heritage information attracts the attention of many researchers and practitioners. A variety of applications can be found for cultural places, such as museums, cities. The focus of this paper is more specially, on World Heritage city guides to be used by locals and tourists to make them understand what makes the WH property outstanding. Some very interesting though non-adaptive mobile guides have been developed over the past years e.g. mTrip, Pocket Guide.

However with the emerging usability of Augmented reality, people can easily find the places where they need to reach. But the current problem is there are still many researches carried out to find the best possible way to give a solution for personalized outdoor tour guides. This project provide such solution for the problem.

1.2 Business Process

My system's business process starts with launching of the Windows Phone 8 and Windows 8 store apps. This system is totally a free service for getting membership and provide low cost shipping facilities. This use targeted ad to earn money.

1.3 Definition of the problem

Personalization is also being a very trending topic since the introduction of Web 2.0. Personalization is just more than welcoming back the user and it is more about giving priorities to his preferences. Personalization gets more attention after Web 2.0 era by the end of 2010s. Emerging social websites were the key factors for personalization in Web 2.0. Personalization has not been limited just for websites but it has made a huge impact on smartphone apps too. Delectable Wine[1] is nearly 4.5 star rated app in iTunes store, available for iPhone, iPad, and iPod touch. This app lets user to capture photos, tag and save wines, users love. This app analyzes what the user loves the most and recommends him or her related ones based on his taste and ratings. Delectable builds a custom "wine profile" of users and makes recommendations based on favorites. This is a very good example of Personalization.

Social network is largely an untapped source of instant, relevant information about users. Social network is a great place to get personalizes content. According to 2013 Consumer Research conducted [2] by Janrain Inc [3] There are a huge number of consumers reports being mis-targeted with ads, offers and promotions. All those consumers mis-targeted because the system is not quite enough to get what user likes. Social logins and Social data make personalization very possible and helpful to target audience with relevant content. Though this is not relevant to the paper, this is a good scenario that is in need of personalization with social data.

Many researches have been revealed how to utilize social network information for a particular system. Almost all social network services provide APIs to integrate in third-party systems as well. The experimental results of the a generic framework for incorporating social context information (about authors' identities and social networks) by Lu al el, show that incorporating social contextual information can help improve the accuracy of review quality prediction especially when the available training data is sparse. The concept "Social Recommender systems" used in this paper is defined as using social friends network to improve recommender systems. We can get more specific context from social networks about a user such as whether (s)he is a student or employee, where does (s)he works or study, where does (s)he lives and his or her personal likes on books, music, sports, food and etc.. This lead us to personalized system.

1.4 Need Analysis

Sri Lankan tourism industry lacks its native technological aspects. Many tourist carries books about Sri Lanka and roam through Sri Lanka. Some tourists depend on Trip Advisor service. But unfortunately all these services and book miss the very crucial places in Sri Lanka. For example, tourist who ever visits to Bambarakanda falls in Sri Lanka, miss the beauty of Belihuloya and Hirikatu owa rivers but these two attractive rivers can be seen on the way to Bambarakanda falls but neither books nor other services never mention about this, so tourists thinks, they need to pay more money to visit those places and they just leave this.

Another problem is about seasonal offers in some tourist places. If you go to Arugambay by later months of the year, you can taste the best Corn. But most tourist miss these offers as well because of the limitations of the existing service.

Here we propose mobile application system that is built on POI manner and provide efficient and

---

[1] https://itunes.apple.com/us/app/delectable-wine/id512106648?mt=8

[2] Details of the report available in http://janrain.com/resources/industry-research/2013-consumer-research-value-of-social-login/

[3] Janrain Inc. is a private technology company that provides software-as-a-service solutions to help organizations improve customer acquisition and intelligence. http://janrain.com/about/

effective service to user. Main users of the system are tourists and local people can user it in their mobile devices as well.

1.5   Aims and objectives

This is an enriching collaboration for project participantsrom both sides as it combines the ideas for indoor and outdoor personalization. Different mechanisms are being used for user positioning for providing recommendations in these environments. GPS or cellular triangulation can be used outdoors. The Excursia outdoor audio guide is GPS enabled; however, these mechanisms do not work indoors. Radio Frequency IDentification (RFID), Wireless Fidelity (Wi–Fi), Bluetooth, Ultra Wide Band (UWB) and Infrared can be used indoors. CHIP provides a small test setup that uses Wi–Fi.

1.6   Scope of the system

Our scope on developing such system is to create an integrated web service that process user preferences and recommend user a good result.

2

System Analysis

2.1 High level diagrams for existing system

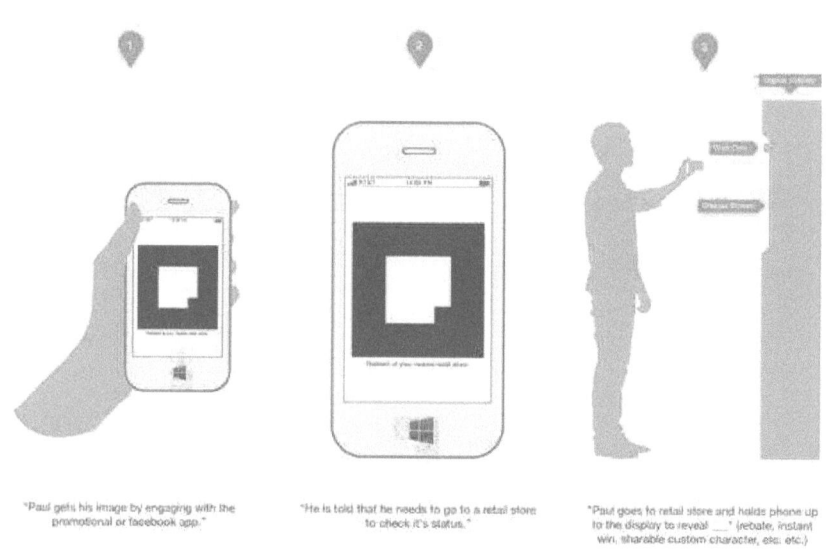

Figure 2.1: Abstract of scenario in users perspective

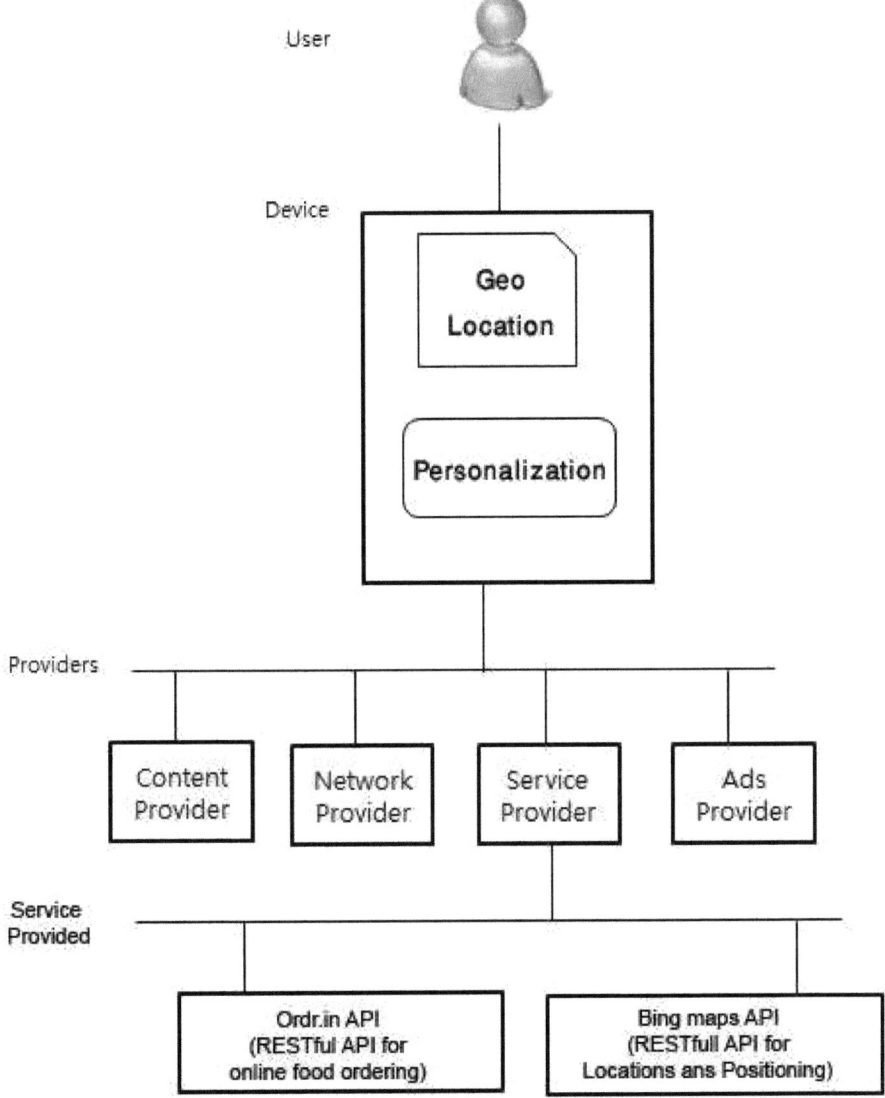

Figure 2.2: Abstract of scenario in systems perspective

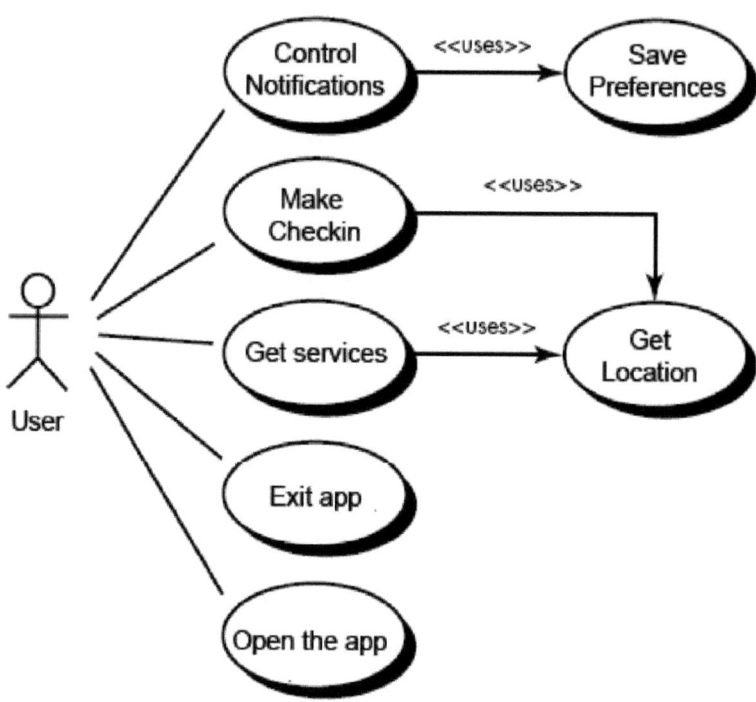

Figure 2.3: Use case diagram for the system

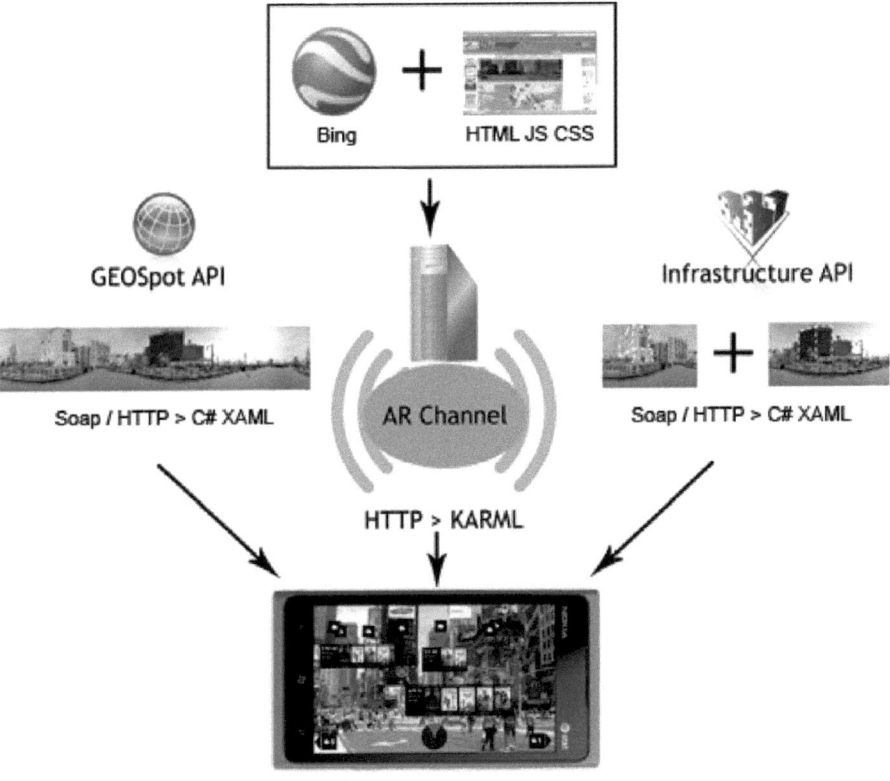

Figure 2.4: How Augmented reality works

2.2 Methodologies used for the system

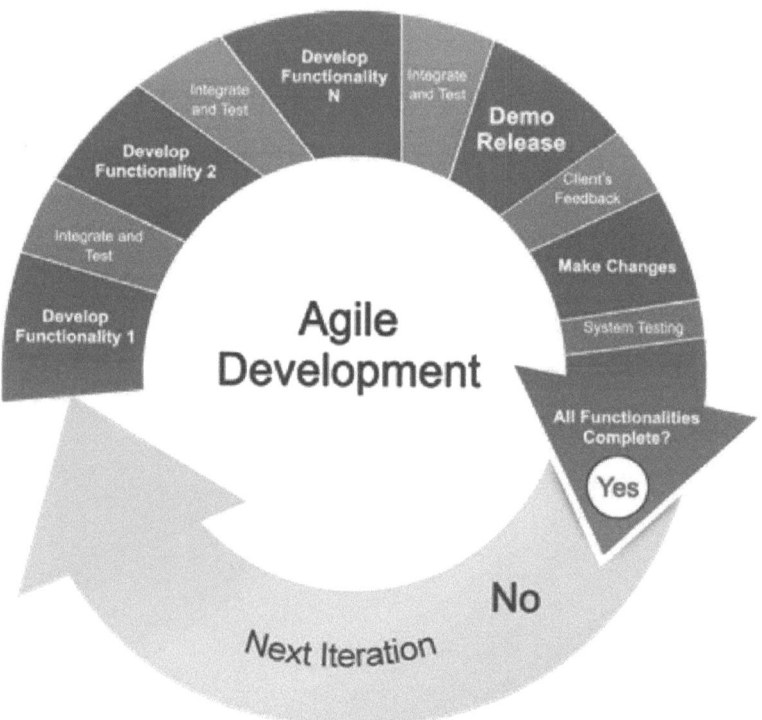

Figure 2.5: Agile Methodology to develop the system

I have used Agile methodology to develop the system, I started with a throw away prototype and expanded our system. Why we started with a throw away prototype is that there are no existing systems like the system, and previously this system was just a concept. We developed our imagination as a simple system and then we study user requirements and more system functionalities needed by our system testers and go through the system.

There are some more other reasons to choose Agile development rather then Water fall model. Actually Traditional Waterfall methodology dictates that scope and features are pinned down ahead of design and implementation. With scope as the unmovable and non-negotiable factor, the other aspects of the project management triad, schedule and cost could then be adjusted accordingly. With Agile methodology, schedule and cost are the major determining factors and it is scope that changes in order to accommodate acceptable business demands.

Using Agile development, iterations provide immediate feedback. Agile methodology calls for smaller release cycles called iterations, in which the product is always in a ready release state. This ready release state is brought about by continuous feedback from product owners and end users with the development and quality assurance team.

Agile development gives us fewer defects in the final product. It is in our nature for humans to be insatiable. We always want more once our most recent craving has been satisfied. It is the same with end users. With the instant feedback that Agile provides, the danger of scope creep comes in. End users who see that requirements can be met "easily" (they see only the result, not the effort) will ask for additional features.

But we faced some problems as well while developing with Agile method. We always want more once our most recent craving has been satisfied. It is the same with end users. With the instant feedback that Agile provides, the danger of scope creep comes in.

Another problem we had was, we started with a requirement and finished with another requirements. Though they satisfy user needs, we feel guilty that our documentation get left behind.

2.3   GUI Design

Figure 2.6: Home page

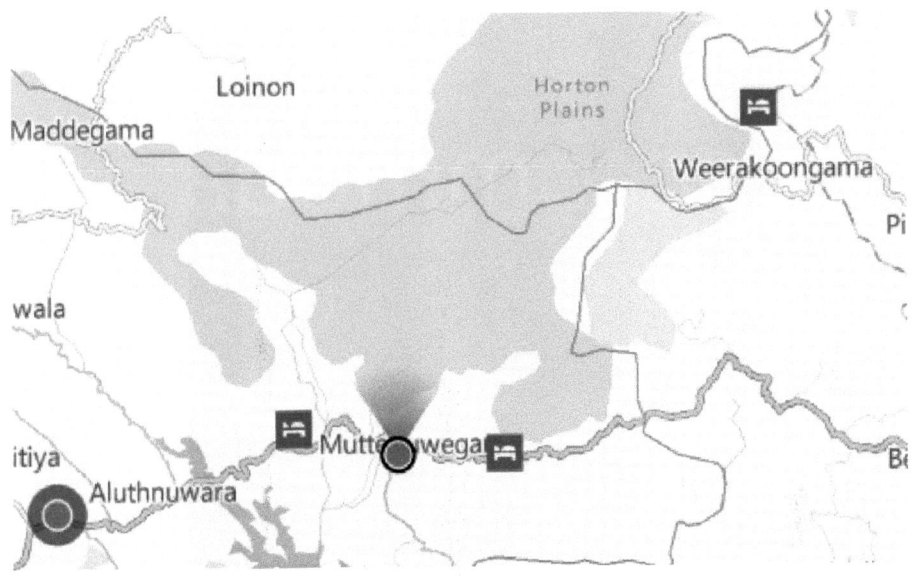

Figure 2.7: System's main map

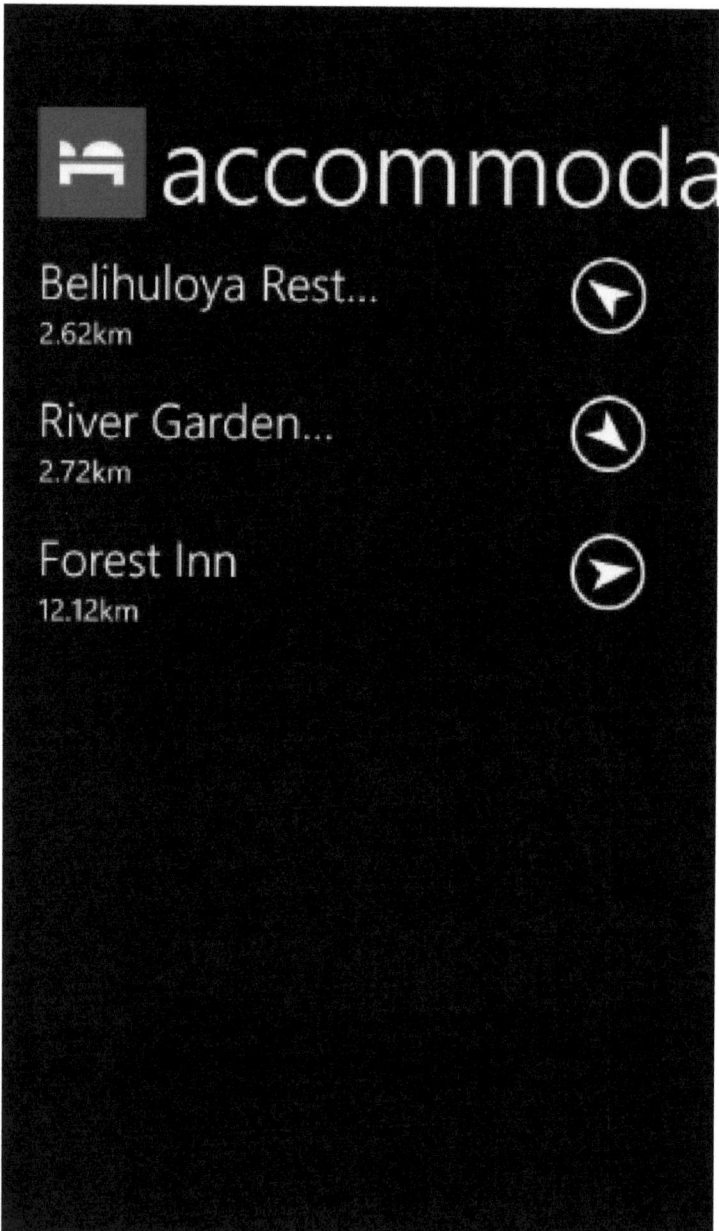

Figure 2.8: System's main map, showing recommended places, nearby

Figure 2.9: Augmented Reality, this uses camera's view port to show the places

Figure 2.10: The app showing a far places which is included in the users preferences

User-interface design of the system start with a prototype and went through some heavy changes. Since we were using C# as our development language, we were using XAML, the markup language used to develop Windows Phone 8 and Windows 8 apps.

XAML (read as Zammel) stands for eXtensible Application Markup Language and it is based on XML (eXtensible Markup Language). XAML is developed by Microsoft to use behind the visual representation of an application. We probably use XAML in Expression Blend or Visual Studio to develop rich media based applications for web and mobile devices. Simply, creating any application in Blend called as writing XAML code either by typing the codes or visually designing and it automatically generates code. Although XAML is developed for use on the Windows platform but the WPF/E (Windows Presentation Foundation/Everywhere) initiative will eventually bring XAML to other platforms and devices.

XAML is based on XML but both are different subject. XML is designed to store data or works with stored data. Microsoft extends the usefulness and power of XML in form of XAML by making it a .NET programming language and extends it lot for us and the result is now here. Now as a developer, you may find yourself scripting XAML tags to write Windows or Web applications. Besides the easy to use and understand, XAML is flexible enough to provide options to use any .NET programming language as code-behind like C#, VB etc. By using XAML, you are not only limited to design UI such as size, color, and layout of Windows but you can also write the events and methods in XAML files.

C# was designed with .NET in mind. That means that it confirms as best to the .NET Common Language Specification of any of the languages. Visual Basic had to be severely redeveloped to fit the spec. It was a "retrofit" of sorts. With that said, there is nothing "wrong" with VB.NET. It's a great language and provides easy transition for people who come from a VB background. C#, however, looks to be developing much faster and provides more powerful featuers that aren't offered by VB.NET. Currently, pointers and Xml Documentation spring to mind as two of the advantages C has over VB.NET. However, if you take a look at the gotdotnet.com C team page, you will see that there are many new features coming to the language. One big one is generics. This is the ability to write classes similar to template classes in C++. I doubt VB.NET will be able to implement this very easy.

A sample XAML comes as follows

```
<Style TargetType="TextBlock">
    <Setter Property="FontSize" Value="25"/>
    <Setter Property="TextWrapping" Value="NoWrap"/>
</Style>

<DataTemplate x:Key="PoiItem">
    <Border BorderBrush="Black" BorderThickness="2" CornerRadius="8"
    Background="#FF003847" Width="250">
        <Grid Margin="4" Tap="PoiItem_Tapped">
            <Grid.ColumnDefinitions>
                <ColumnDefinition Width="Auto"/>
                <ColumnDefinition Width="0.5*"/>
            </Grid.ColumnDefinitions>
            <Grid.RowDefinitions>
                <RowDefinition/>
                <RowDefinition/>
                <RowDefinition/>
            </Grid.RowDefinitions>

            <Image Grid.RowSpan="3" Source="{Binding EntityTypeID,
            Converter={StaticResource EntityIconConverter}}"
            Stretch="Uniform" MaxHeight="50"
            HorizontalAlignment="Center"
            VerticalAlignment="Center" Margin="0,0,10,0"/>

            <TextBlock Text="{Binding Name}" Grid.Column="1"/>
            <TextBlock Text="{Binding EntityTypeID,
            Converter={StaticResource EntityNameConverter}}"
            Grid.Row="1" Grid.Column="1"/>

            <StackPanel Orientation="Horizontal" Grid.Row="2" Grid.Column="1">
```

```
            <TextBlock Text="{Binding Distance}"/>
            <TextBlock Text=" meters"/>
        </StackPanel>
      </Grid>
    </Border>
</DataTemplate>
```

Other controlling parts are done through C# as follows

```
private void PoiItem_Tapped(object sender, System.Windows.Input.GestureEventArgs e)
{
    ARItem selectedItem = null;

    if (sender is Grid)
    {
        selectedItem = (sender as Grid).DataContext as ARItem;

        //Check to see if the item is already selected. If so then toggle it.
        if (selectedItem == SelectedItem)
        {
            selectedItem = null;
        }
    }

    if (sender is Ellipse)
    {
        selectedItem = (sender as Ellipse).Tag as ARItem;
    }

    SetSelectedItem(selectedItem);
}

private void Directions_Tapped(object sender, System.Windows.Input.GestureEventArgs e)
{
    if (SelectedItem != null)
    {
        var poiItem = SelectedItem as PoiItem;

        MapsDirectionsTask directionTask = new MapsDirectionsTask()
        {
            Start = new LabeledMapLocation("My Location", ARDisplay.Location),
            End = new LabeledMapLocation(poiItem.Name, poiItem.GeoLocation)
        };
```

```
        directionTask.Show();
    }
}

private void Share_Tapped(object sender, System.Windows.Input.GestureEventArgs e)
{
    if (SelectedItem != null)
    {
        var poiItem = SelectedItem as PoiItem;

        //Create a converter for converting the Entity Type ID of the
        selected item to a user friendly text.
        BingMapsAR.Converters.EntityTypeNameConverter converter
        = new BingMapsAR.Converters.EntityTypeNameConverter();

        EmailComposeTask emailComposeTask = new EmailComposeTask()
        {
            Subject = poiItem.Name,
            Body = string.Format("{0} - {1}\r\n{2}, {3} {4}\r\nPhone: {5}",
            poiItem.Name, converter.Convert(poiItem.EntityTypeID, null, null, null),
            poiItem.AddressLine, poiItem.Locality, poiItem.PostalCode, poiItem.Phone)
        };

        emailComposeTask.Show();
    }
}
```

2.4   Program Design

Under program design we have considered the following concepts to develop the system

- Compatibility - The software is able to operate with other products that are designed for inter-operability with another product. For example, a piece of software may be backward-compatible with an older version of itself.

- Extensibility - New capabilities can be added to the software without major changes to the underlying architecture.

- Fault-tolerance - The software is resistant to and able to recover from component failure.

- Maintainability - A measure of how easily bug fixes or functional modifications can be accomplished. High maintainability can be the product of modularity and extensibility.

- Modularity - the resulting software comprises well defined, independent components. That leads to better maintainability. The components could be then implemented and tested in isolation before being integrated to form a desired software system. This allows division of work in a software development project.

- Reliability - The software is able to perform a required function under stated conditions for a specified period of time.

- Reusability - the software is able to add further features and modification with slight or no modification.

- Robustness - The software is able to operate under stress or tolerate unpredictable or invalid input. For example, it can be designed with a resilience to low memory conditions.

- Security - The software is able to withstand hostile acts and influences.

- Usability - The software user interface must be usable for its target user/audience. Default values for the parameters must be chosen so that they are a good choice for the majority of the users.

- Performance - The software performs its tasks within a user-acceptable time. The software does not consume too much memory.

3

System Development

3.1 Brief description about the Developing environment tools & programming language

I have used C# and XAML to develop my system client apps on both Windows Phone and Windows 8 platforms.

XAML is a declarative language that you can use to create application UI such as controls, shapes, text, and other content presented on the screen. If you're familiar with web programming, you can think of XAML as similar to HTML. Like HTML, XAML is made up of elements and attributes. But XAML is XML-based and therefore must follow XML rules, which include being well-formed. You might ask, "Why do I care about XAML if I'm just going to use tools like Microsoft Visual Studio or Blend for Visual Studio to create the UI?" Even though there are tools that generate markup, you'll invariably want to go under the covers to understand or tweak the XAML. Besides, sometimes it's just easier to code UI by hand when you want fine control or just want to know what's going on.

One aspect of using a declarative language like XAML is having some separation between the markup that makes up the UI and the code that makes the application do something. For example, a designer on your team could design a UI and then hand off the XAML to the developer to add the procedural code. Even if the designer and the developer are the same person (as they often are), you can keep your visuals in XAML files (.xaml) and your procedural UI code in code-behind files (.cs and .vb).

Microsoft Visual Studio is an integrated development environment (IDE) from Microsoft. It is used to develop computer programs for Microsoft Windows superfamily of operating systems, as well as web sites, web applications and web services. Visual Studio uses Microsoft software development platforms such as Windows API, Windows Forms, Windows Presentation Foundation, Windows Store and Microsoft Silverlight. It can produce both native code and managed code.

Visual Studio includes a code editor supporting IntelliSense as well as code refactoring. The integrated debugger works both as a source-level debugger and a machine-level debugger. Other built-in tools include a forms designer for building GUI applications, web designer, class designer, and database schema designer. It accepts plug-ins that enhance the functionality at almost every level—including adding support for source-control systems (like Subversion) and adding new toolsets like editors and visual designers for domain-specific languages or toolsets for other aspects of the software development lifecycle (like the Team Foundation Server client: Team Explorer).

Visual Studio includes a debugger that works both as a source-level debugger and as a machine-level debugger. It works with both managed code as well as native code and can be used for debugging applications written in any language supported by Visual Studio. In addition, it can also attach to running processes and monitor and debug those processes. If source code for the running process is available, it displays the code as it is being run. If source code is not available, it can show the disassembly. The Visual Studio debugger can also create memory dumps as well as load them later for debugging. Multi-threaded programs are also supported. The debugger can be configured to be launched when an application running outside the Visual Studio environment crashes.

The debugger allows setting breakpoints (which allow execution to be stopped temporarily at a certain position) and watches (which monitor the values of variables as the execution progresses). Breakpoints can be conditional, meaning they get triggered when the condition is met. Code can be stepped over, i.e., run one line (of source code) at a time. It can either step into functions to debug inside it, or step over it, i.e., the execution of the function body isn't available for manual inspection. The debugger supports Edit and Continue, i.e., it allows code to be edited as it is being debugged (32 bit only; not supported in 64 bit). When debugging, if the mouse pointer hovers over any variable, its current value is displayed in a tooltip ('data tooltips"), where it can also be modified if desired. During coding, the Visual Studio debugger lets certain functions be invoked manually from the Immediate tool window. The parameters to the method are supplied at the Immediate window.

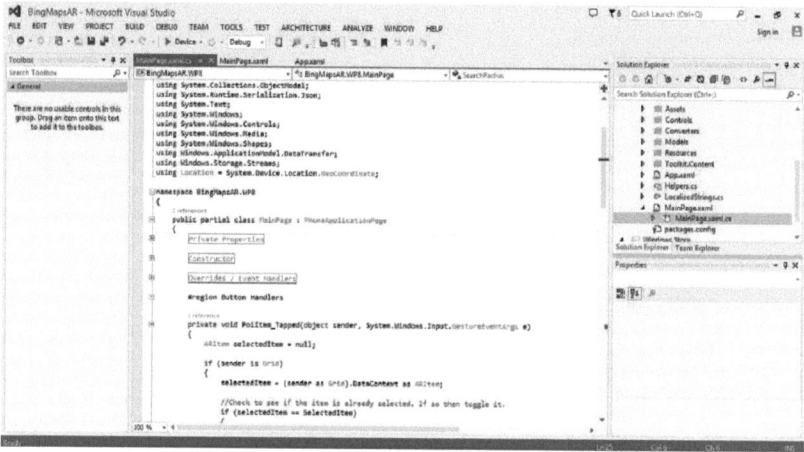

Figure 3.1: Visual Studio 2013

Figure 3.2: Sample XAML code, coded in Visual Studio 2013

3.2 Security Infrastructure

The proposed system that we are going to develop will be used as the Chief performance system for providing help to the organization in managing the whole database of the student studying in the organization. Therefore, it is expected that the database would perform functionally all the requirements that are specified We are going to develop a secured database.

I have developed this app to save user preferences in a secure manner. Which is encrypted by hash algorithms. The procedure to save and load such user preferences using IsolatedStorageSettings class. It provides a dictionary-like, key-value store which is preserved across device reboots. The settings are securely stored inside the Isolated Storage space of an application, and are inaccessible to other applications.

3.3 Data Structures & Algorithms used in the system

We have used hash table data structures specially MD5 hases used to store user preferences.

3.4 Implementation of Algorithm

We have used hash table data structures specially MD5 hases used to store passwords to the database. The code snippet comes like the below

```
using System;
```

```csharp
using System.Security.Cryptography;
using System.Text;

namespace MD5Sample
{
    class Program
    {
        static string GetMd5Hash(MD5 md5Hash, string input)
        {
            // Convert the input string to a
            // byte array and compute the hash.
            byte[] data =
            md5Hash.ComputeHash(Encoding.UTF8.GetBytes(input));

            // Create a new Stringbuilder to collect the bytes
            // and create a string.
            StringBuilder sBuilder = new StringBuilder();

            // Loop through each byte of the hashed data
            // and format each one as a hexadecimal string.
            for (int i = 0; i < data.Length; i++)
            {
                sBuilder.Append(data[i].ToString("x2"));
            }

            // Return the hexadecimal string.
            return sBuilder.ToString();
        }

        // Verify a hash against a string.
        static bool VerifyMd5Hash(MD5 md5Hash, string input, string hash)
        {
            // Hash the input.
            string hashOfInput = GetMd5Hash(md5Hash, input);

            // Create a StringComparer an compare the hashes.
            StringComparer comparer = StringComparer.OrdinalIgnoreCase;

            if (0 == comparer.Compare(hashOfInput, hash))
            {
                return true;
            }
```

```
            else
            {
                return false;
            }
        }
    }
}
```

3.5   Augmented Reality Algorithm

Augmented reality (AR) is a live direct or indirect view of a physical, real-world environment whose elements are augmented (or supplemented) by computer-generated sensory input such as sound, video, graphics or GPS data. It is related to a more general concept called mediated reality, in which a view of reality is modified (possibly even diminished rather than augmented) by a computer. As a result, the technology functions by enhancing one's current perception of reality. By contrast, virtual reality replaces the real world with a simulated one. Augmentation is conventionally in real-time and in semantic context with environmental elements, such as sports scores on TV during a match. With the help of advanced AR technology (e.g. adding computer vision and object recognition) the information about the surrounding real world of the user becomes interactive and digitally manipulable. Artificial information about the environment and its objects can be overlaid on the real world.

We can use the Motion API to create Windows Phone applications that use the device's orientation and movement in space as an input mechanism. The Windows Phone platform includes APIs to obtain raw sensor data from the device's Compass, Gyroscope, and Accelerometer sensors. However the Motion API handles the complex math necessary to combine the data from these sensors and produce easy-to-use values for the device's attitude and motion.

The below code used to program the Augmented Reality for the system

```
using System.Windows;

#if WINDOWS_PHONE
using Microsoft.Phone.Controls;
using System.Device.Location;
using System.Windows.Controls;
using System.Windows.Media;
using VideoSource = System.Windows.Media.Brush;
#endif

#if WP7
using Microsoft.Phone.Controls.Maps.Platform;
#endif

#if WP8
using Microsoft.Phone.Maps.Controls;
```

```
using Location = System.Device.Location.GeoCoordinate;
#endif

#if WIN_RT
using Bing.Maps;
using Windows.Devices.Geolocation;
using Windows.UI.Xaml;
using Windows.UI.Xaml.Controls;
using Windows.UI.Xaml.Media;
using VideoSource = Windows.Media.Capture.MediaCapture;
#endif

using GART.BaseControls;
using GART.Data;
#if X3D
using GART.X3D;
using Matrix = GART.X3D.Matrix;
#else
using Microsoft.Xna.Framework;
using Matrix = Microsoft.Xna.Framework.Matrix;
#endif
using System.Collections.ObjectModel;
using System.ComponentModel;

namespace GART.Controls
{
    /// <summary>
    /// A base control that serves as the starting point
    for an augmented reality view that renders ARItems.
    /// </summary>
    #if WINDOWS_PHONE
    public abstract class ARItemsView : ListBox, IARItemsView
    #endif
    #if WIN_RT
    public abstract class ARItemsView : ListView, IARItemsView
    #endif
    {
        #region Static Version
        #region Dependency Properties
        /// <summary>
        /// Identifies the <see cref="ARItems"/> dependency property.
        /// </summary>
        static public readonly DependencyProperty ARItemsProperty =
```

```
DependencyProperty.Register("ARItems",
  typeof(ObservableCollection<ARItem>),
   typeof(ARItemsView),
   new PropertyMetadata(new ObservableCollection<ARItem>(),
    OnARItemsChanged));

private static void OnARItemsChanged
(DependencyObject d, DependencyPropertyChangedEventArgs e)
{
    ((ARItemsView)d).OnARItemsChanged(e);
}

/// <summary>
/// Identifies the <see cref="Attitude"/> dependency property.
/// </summary>
static public readonly DependencyProperty AttitudeProperty =
 DependencyProperty.Register("Attitude",
 typeof(Matrix), typeof(ARItemsView),
 new PropertyMetadata(ARDefaults.EmptyMatrix,
  OnAttitudeChanged));

private static void OnAttitudeChanged
(DependencyObject d, DependencyPropertyChangedEventArgs e)
{
    ((ARItemsView)d).OnAttitudeChanged(e);
}

/// <summary>
/// Identifies the <see cref="AttitudeHeading"/> dependency property.
/// </summary>
static public readonly DependencyProperty AttitudeHeadingProperty =
 DependencyProperty.Register("AttitudeHeading",
  typeof(double), typeof(ARItemsView),
   new PropertyMetadata(0d,
    OnAttitudeHeadingChanged));

private static void OnAttitudeHeadingChanged
(DependencyObject d, DependencyPropertyChangedEventArgs e)
{
    ((ARItemsView)d).OnAttitudeHeadingChanged(e);
}

/// <summary>
```

```
/// Identifies the <see cref="Location"/> dependency property.
/// </summary>
static public readonly DependencyProperty LocationProperty =
DependencyProperty.Register("Location",
 typeof(Location),
  typeof(ARItemsView),
   new
   PropertyMetadata
   (ARDefaults.DefaultStartLocation, OnLocationChanged));

private static void OnLocationChanged
(DependencyObject d, DependencyPropertyChangedEventArgs e)
{
    ((ARItemsView)d).OnLocationChanged(e);
}

/// <summary>
/// Identifies the <see cref="Orientation"/> dependency property
/// </summary>
static public DependencyProperty OrientationProperty =
DependencyProperty.Register("Orientation",
 typeof(ControlOrientation),
  typeof(ARItemsView), new PropertyMetadata(ControlOrientation.Default,
  OnOrientationChanged));

private static void OnOrientationChanged
(DependencyObject d, DependencyPropertyChangedEventArgs e)
{
    ((ARItemsView)d).OnOrientationChanged(e);
}

/// <summary>
/// Identifies the <see cref="TravelHeading"/> dependency property.
/// </summary>
static public readonly DependencyProperty TravelHeadingProperty =
DependencyProperty.Register("TravelHeading",
 typeof(double),
 typeof(ARItemsView),
  new PropertyMetadata
  (0d, OnTravelHeadingChanged));

private static void OnTravelHeadingChanged
(DependencyObject d, DependencyPropertyChangedEventArgs e)
```

```
{
    ((ARItemsView)d).OnTravelHeadingChanged(e);
}


/// <summary>
/// Identifies the <see cref="VideoSource"/> dependency property.
/// </summary>
static public readonly DependencyProperty VideoSourceProperty
= DependencyProperty.Register("VideoSource",
 typeof(VideoSource),
  typeof(ARItemsView),
   new PropertyMetadata
   (ARDefaults.DefaultVideoSource,
    OnVideoSourceChanged));

private static void OnVideoSourceChanged
(DependencyObject d, DependencyPropertyChangedEventArgs e)
{
    ((ARItemsView)d).OnVideoSourceChanged(e);
}


#endregion // Dependency Properties
#endregion // Static Version

#region Instance Version
#region Overridables / Event Triggers

protected virtual void OnOrientationChanged
(DependencyPropertyChangedEventArgs e)
{
}


/// <summary>
/// Occurs when the value of the <see cref="ARItems"/> property has changed.
/// </summary>
/// <param name="e">
/// A <see cref="DependencyPropertyChangedEventArgs"/>
/// containing event information.
/// </param>
protected virtual void OnARItemsChanged(DependencyPropertyChangedEventArgs e)
{
    // Change our ItemsSource to be the new items collection
    this.ItemsSource = this.ARItems;
```

```
}

/// <summary>
/// Occurs when the value of the <see cref="Attitude"/> property has changed.
/// </summary>
/// <param name="e">
/// A <see cref="DependencyPropertyChangedEventArgs"/>

///containing event information.
/// </param>
protected virtual void OnAttitudeChanged
(DependencyPropertyChangedEventArgs e)
{

}

/// <summary>
/// Occurs when the value of the <see cref="AttitudeHeading"/>
///property has changed.
/// </summary>
/// <param name="e">
/// A <see cref="DependencyPropertyChangedEventArgs"/>
/// containing event information.
/// </param>
protected virtual void OnAttitudeHeadingChanged
(DependencyPropertyChangedEventArgs e)
{

}

/// <summary>
/// Occurs when the value of the <see cref="Location"/> property has changed.
/// </summary>
/// <param name="e">
/// A <see cref="DependencyPropertyChangedEventArgs"/>
/// containing event information.
/// </param>
protected virtual void OnLocationChanged
(DependencyPropertyChangedEventArgs e)
{

}
```

```
/// <summary>
/// Occurs when the value of the <see cref="TravelHeading"/> property
///has changed.
/// </summary>
/// <param name="e">
/// A <see cref="DependencyPropertyChangedEventArgs"/> containing event
///information.
/// </param>
protected virtual void OnTravelHeadingChanged
(DependencyPropertyChangedEventArgs e)
{

}

/// <summary>
/// Occurs when the value of the <see cref="VideoBrush"/> property has changed.
/// </summary>
/// <param name="e">
/// A <see cref="DependencyPropertyChangedEventArgs"/>
 containing event information.
/// </param>
protected virtual void OnVideoSourceChanged
(DependencyPropertyChangedEventArgs e)
{

}
#endregion // Overridables / Event Triggers

#region Public Properties
/// <summary>
/// Gets or sets the collection of ARItems rendered by the view.
///This is a dependency property.
/// </summary>
/// <value>
/// The collection of ARItems rendered by the view.
/// </value>
#if WP7
[Category("AR")]
#endif
public ObservableCollection<ARItem> ARItems
{
    get
    {
```

```
            return (ObservableCollection<ARItem>)GetValue(ARItemsProperty);
        }
        set
        {
            SetValue(ARItemsProperty, value);
        }
    }

    /// <summary>
    /// Gets or sets a matrix that represents where the user is looking.
    ///This is a dependency property.
    /// </summary>
    /// <value>
    /// A matrix that represents where the user is looking.
    /// </value>
    #if WP7
    [Category("AR")]
    #endif
    public Matrix Attitude
    {
        get
        {
            return (Matrix)GetValue(AttitudeProperty);
        }
        set
        {
            SetValue(AttitudeProperty, value);
        }
    }

    /// <summary>
    /// Gets or sets the direction the user is looking in degrees.
    /// This is a dependency property.
    /// </summary>
    /// <value>
    /// The direction the user is looking in degrees.
    /// </value>
    #if WP7
    [Category("AR")]
    #endif
    public double AttitudeHeading
    {
        get
```

```
        {
            return (double)GetValue(AttitudeHeadingProperty);
        }
        set
        {
            SetValue(AttitudeHeadingProperty, value);
        }
}

/// <summary>
/// Gets or sets the location of the user in Geo space.
/// This is a dependency property.
/// </summary>
/// <value>
/// The location of the user in Geo space.
/// </value>
#if WP7
[Category("AR")]
#endif
public Location Location
{
    get
    {
        return (Location)GetValue(LocationProperty);
    }
    set
    {
        SetValue(LocationProperty, value);
    }
}


/// <summary>
/// Gets or sets current device orientation
/// </summary>
/// <value>
/// Current <see cref="PageOrientation"/> of a device
/// </value>
#if WP7
[Category("AR")]
#endif
public ControlOrientation Orientation
{
```

```
        get { return (ControlOrientation)GetValue(OrientationProperty); }
        set { SetValue(OrientationProperty, value); }
}

/// <summary>
/// Gets or sets the direction the user is traveling in degrees.
/// This is a dependency property.
/// </summary>
/// <value>
/// The direction the user is traveling in degrees.
/// </value>
#if WP7
[Category("AR")]
#endif
public double TravelHeading
{
    get
    {
        return (double)GetValue(TravelHeadingProperty);
    }
    set
    {
        SetValue(TravelHeadingProperty, value);
    }
}

/// <summary>
/// Gets or sets the video source for the camera.
/// This is a dependency property.
/// </summary>
/// <value>
/// The video source for the camera.
/// </value>
#if WP7
[Category("AR")]
#endif
public VideoSource VideoSource
{
    get
    {
        return (VideoSource)GetValue(VideoSourceProperty);
    }
    set
```

```
            {
                SetValue(VideoSourceProperty, value);
            }
        }
        #endregion // Public Properties

        #endregion // Instance Version
    }
}
```

3.6   Saving User Preferences

The following algorithm can be used to save, edit and retrieve user preferences.

```
private void btnSave_Click(object sender, RoutedEventArgs e)
{
    IsolatedStorageSettings settings = IsolatedStorageSettings.ApplicationSettings;
    // txtInput is a TextBox defined in XAML.
    if (!settings.Contains("userData"))
    {
        settings.Add("userData", txtInput.Text);
    }
    else
    {
        settings["userData"] = txtInput.Text;
    }
    settings.Save();
}

private void btnDisplay_Click(object sender, RoutedEventArgs e)
{
    // txtDisplay is a TextBlock defined in XAML.
    txtDisplay.Text = "USER DATA: ";
    if (IsolatedStorageSettings.ApplicationSettings.Contains("userData"))
    {
        txtDisplay.Text +=
        IsolatedStorageSettings.ApplicationSettings["userData"] as string;
    }
}

private void btnRemove_Click(object sender, RoutedEventArgs e)
{
    if (IsolatedStorageSettings.ApplicationSettings.Contains("userData"))
```

```
    {
        IsolatedStorageSettings.ApplicationSettings.Remove("userData");
    }
}
```

4

System Testing

4.1 Testing methodology used

We have used V model to test ur system

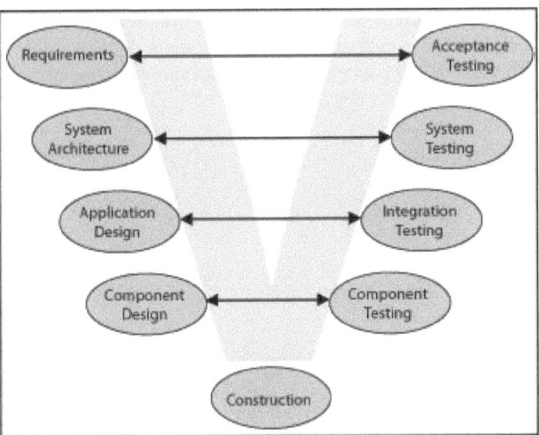

Figure 4.1: V model testing

We used V model testing because its very simple and easier to implement. Testing activities like planning, test designing happens well before coding. This saves a lot of time. Hence higher chance of success over the waterfall model. It avoids the downward flow of the defects as well.

In the basic Waterfall model process seen some disadvantages or limitations in the model which started a new SDLC model. As we seen in the Waterfall model the issues found in the end of the SDLC, this is due to the testing is occurred in the end phases of the you SDLC. To overcome this problem the V-Model is comes into the picture. It is always better to introduce testing in the early phase of SDLC, as in this model the testing activity gets started from the early phase of the SDLC.

Before starting the actual testing, testing team has to work on various activities like preparation of Test Strategy, Test Planning, Creation of Test cases & Test Scripts which is work parallel with the development activity which help to get the test deliverable on time.

In the V Model Software Development Life Cycle, based on same information(requirement specification document) the development & testing activity is started. Based on the requirement document developer team started working on the design & after completion on design start actual implementation and testing team starts working on test planning, test case writing, test scripting. Both activities are working parallel to each other. In Waterfall model & V-model they are quite similar to each other. As it is most popular Software Testing Life Cycle model so most of the organization is following this model.

The V-model is also called as Verification and Validation model. The testing activity is perform in the each phase of Software Testing Life Cycle phase. In the first half of the model validations testing activity is integrated in each phase like review user requirements, System Design document & in the next half the Verification testing activity is come in picture.

Typical V-model shows Software Development activities on the Left hand side of model and the Right hand side of the model actual Testing Phases can be performed.

In this process "Do-Procedure" would be followed by the developer team and the "Check-Procedure" would be followed by the testing team to meets the mentioned requirements.

4.2 Test cases and Test results

Date				2014 June 1		
System				Nokia Lumia 820 with Windos Phone 8		
Objective				To test whether the system saves, manipulate preferences		
Version or Release				3 rd proto type (Version 0.03)		
Tested by				MI Isham Mohamed		
ID	Description	Action	Test Data	Expected Results	Result	Comments
1	Open app	Tap the app icon in startscreen		App opens	Pass	
2	Save preferences	Give sample user preference data	User's preferred hotel/	Settings should be saved	Pass	
3	Check recommendation	Put the phone to idle more until it reached the proffered lunch notification time		Notification alert pop-ups	Pass	
4	Edit one preference	Launch edit preferences page to edit it.	New settings data	Settings edited successfully	Pass	
5	Delete one preference	Launch the preferences page and try to delete one preference		A successfull message after deletion	Pass	If username and password are wrong this will be fail

Table 4.1: Test case on saving and manipulating user preferences

Date			2014 June 1			
System			Nokia Lumia 820 phone with Windows Phone 8			
Objective			To test whether Augmented reality works correctly			
Version or Release			3 rd proto type (Version 0.03)			
Tested by			MI Isham Mohamed			
ID	Description	Action	Test Data	Expected Results	Result	Comments
1	Open app	Tap app icon on startscreen		App opens	Pass	
2	View Camera	The Augmented reality feature will automatically suggest you the palces in Camera view port	Location co-ordinates	It should show some places	Pass	If there is no nearest places which are in preferences this will not show places

Table 4.2: Testing Augmented Reality

5

System Implementation

5.1 Implementation Requirements

After an organization makes a commitment to make its app accessible, it is important to plan for implementation of accessibility. This page lists detailed considerations for the planning process, followed by resource pages with more information. Actual implementation plans, as well as the optimal order of the steps, will vary from organization to organization.

- Establish Responsibilities.
- Develop Organizational Policy.
- Select Software for internal organization.
- Provide Training for cooperate workers.
- Promote Organizational Awareness.
- Monitor App accessibility.
- Arrange Public awareness programs.

After global implementation of the system will be available in Windows Phone store. Though this domain exist now, we have a plan to buy that domain.

5.2 Installation guide

Since the system is an app, you can install this from Windows Phone store. Installing is easy, users have to search from the store and install the app.

5.3 User manual

Launch
Open the app

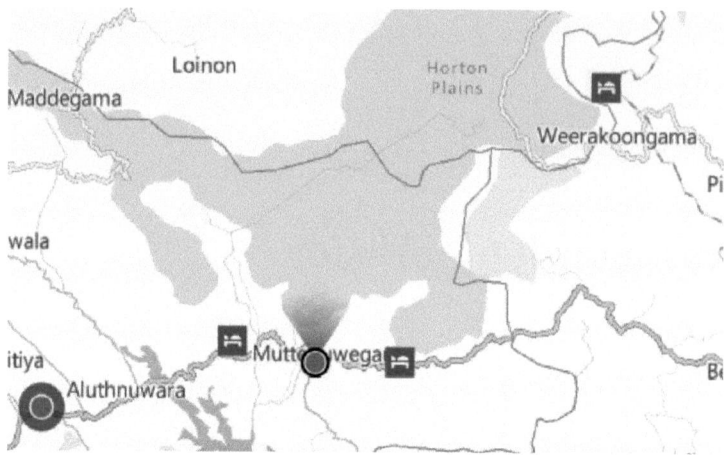

Figure 5.1: Main screen of the app on launched.

By tapping the map user can get the listed of places where he saved in preferences.

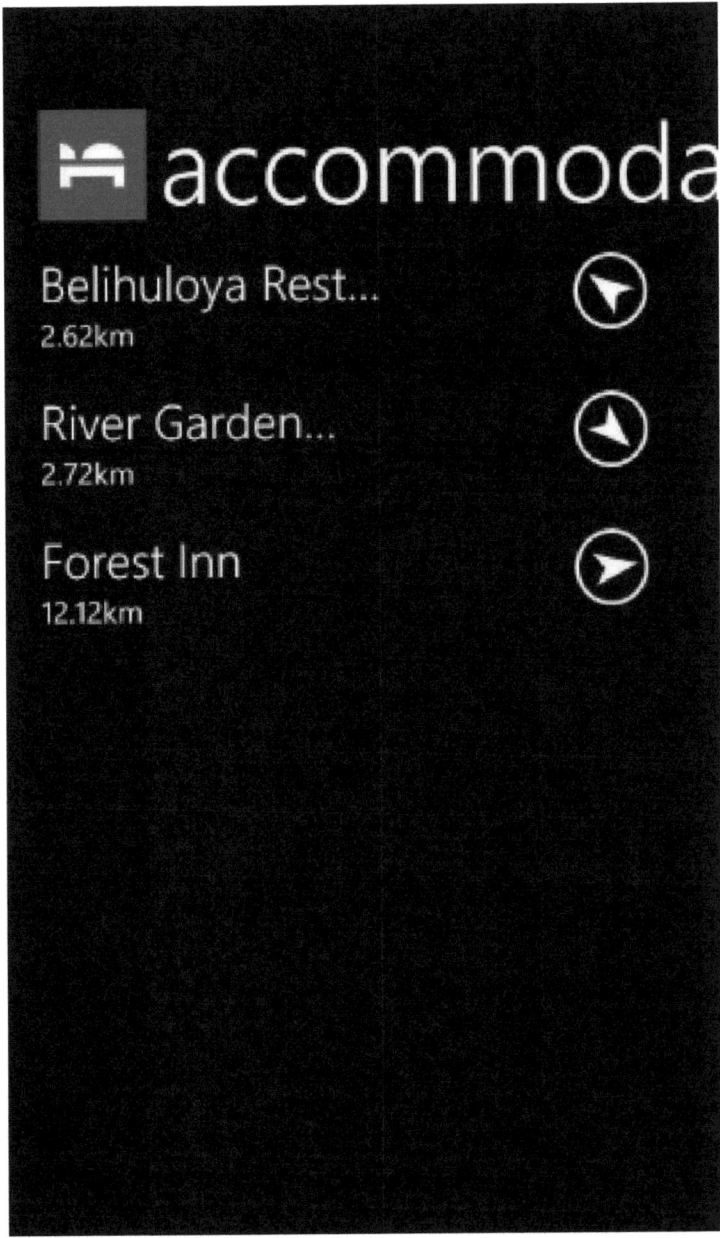

Figure 5.2: Showing the palces which are listed in user preferences

Tap a place to show it in Augmented reality view.

Figure 5.3: Showing a place

Tap pause button to back to the list again

Figure 5.4: Showing the list again

Tap another place to show it in Augmented reality view.

Figure 5.5: Showing another place

5.4 User Training

End users doesn't need any special training on this but watch dog employees need to be trained to access the database and filter contents.

6

Discussion & Conclusion

6.1 The degree of objectives met

Today there are several apps available to fulfill the needs but still tourist, particularly when they spend their time in Sri Lanka, they still use books about Sri Lanka because the non-reliable information available in existing apps like trip-advisor. Those apps does not focus all places in Sri Lanka, as I said early, places like Hirikatoya river are never mentioned in the trip advisor and other existing online services as well. So we need to feed the places, almost all places in Sri Lanka in the online API service we are using. Those services provide interfaces to feed our custom places as well.

We need to develop a database that maintains data about seasonal offers and festivals in Sri Lanka as well. This is will truly be a beneficial for tourist.

6.2 Usability, Accessibility, Reliability and User friendliness of the system

This is a very simple system we have implemented a minimal design rather then focusing big objects, images, videos with red green and blue colours. Thus this system is easier to use on the go. Since we have implemented a minimal UI this used a very small ammount of System resources and Internet data.

This system is built up on the most reliable existing technology. Cloud servers are very hard to crack and hack. We have used 2 layer MD5 hash so password guessing too hard for hackers. Since C# manages its own garbage collecting works this is a very reliable platform with fault tolerance.

6.3 Limitations and Drawbacks

There are some limitations in the system that some tourist places in Sri Lanka and other countires which are located in hard to reach places are not includeded in the location services.

6.4 Further Modification and Enhancement

In future there may be more reliable technologies to come and we are looking forward to them to get used in the system. We are set to develop Android, iOS, Windows Phone and Windows 8 apps for the system.

6.5 Conclusion

The aim of the proposed project is to build a semantic recommender for outdoor guides which utilizes knowledge about a particular user, statistics and current context (e.g. location, visited places, time, date, day of week, weather, etc.) for dynamic creation of personalized routes through the most interesting points in an area.

Prototypes of server and client platforms are implemented in Java. Test content coverage is ready for Saint-Petersburg and Helsinki. The basic product is in a closed beta stage.

Hard−coded recommendations are already available. In every area (city), the user may choose preferred topics from a list. Based on this selection, location and links amongst POIs dened by content creator, this software can give personal recommendations on where to go next. Still all these recommendations are static. A user model and semantic technologies are not yet involved. So more advanced recommender features are under development.

Bibliography

[1] Francesco Ricci, Lior Rokach, Bracha Shapira, Paul B. Kantor, *Recommender Systems Handbook* . Springer, 2011 edition (October 29, 2010), ISBN-10: 0387858199, ISBN-13: 978-0387858197.

[2] Alexey Koren, Natalia Stash, Alexander Andreev, *A Proposal for Semantic Recommender for Outdoor Audio Tour Guides*. ACM Recommender Systems, 2011, Chicago, IL, USA.

[3] Telles. R, Guimaraes.A, Macedo.H, *Automated feeding of POI base for the generation of route descriptions*. Telematics and Information Systems (EATIS), 2012 6th Euro American Conference, May 23–25 2012, ISBN: 978-1-4503-1012-3, IEEE.

[4] Hao Ma, Dengyong Zhou, Chao Liu, Michael R. Lyu, Irwin King, *Recommender Systems with Social Regularization*. WSDM'11, February 9–12, 2011, Hong Kong, China.

[5] Applying Behavioral Principles to Personalize Content Using Social Media, http://www.uxmatters.com/mt/archives/2013/08/applying-behavioral-principles-to-personalize-content-using-social-media.php, August 19, 2013.

[6] How Online Personalization Can Create Compelling Customer Experiences and Build a Better Business, http://blog.kissmetrics.com/online-personalization/, May 4, 2014.

[7] Social Data Matters, http://digiday.com/agencies/social-data-matters/, May 4, 2014.

Printed by Books on Demand GmbH, Norderstedt / Germany